The Title-Page
of the
First Folio of
Shakespeare's Plays

The Title-Page

of the

First Folio of Shakespeare's Plays

A Comparative Study of the

Droeshout Portrait and the Stratford Monument

by

M. H. SPIELMANN, F.S.A.

Written for

THE SHAKESPEARE ASSOCIATION

in celebration of

THE FIRST FOLIO TERCENTENARY

1923

LONDON
HUMPHREY MILFORD
OXFORD UNIVERSITY PRESS
1924

PRINTED IN ENGLAND
AT THE OXFORD UNIVERSITY PRESS
BY FREDERICK HALL

To

Sir *ISRAEL GOLLANCZ, Litt.D., F.B.A.*

Scholar and Friend

This brief Study is

Inscribed.

PREFATORY NOTE

THE occasion and purpose which this Lecture was designed to serve naturally preclude consideration of the subject in the more extended form necessary for exhaustive exposition. Yet for the general reader it is perhaps full enough. It is presented here as it was delivered, but with a number of emendations, additions, and notes which seemed to be desirable.

Cordial thanks are expressed to Mr. H. C. Folger, Mr. Beatson Blair, Sir James R. Fergusson, Bart., Dr. William Martin, Mr. Frederick W. MacMonnies, and Professor Charles J. Allen; to Bodley's Librarian, the Warden of Wadham College, Oxford, the Committees of the Manchester Corporation Art Gallery and the Shakespeare Memorial at Stratford-on-Avon, for authority to reproduce the works pictured in the following pages. I am also indebted for further gracious permissions to the late Lady Guendolen Ramsden, the late Earl of Warwick, and the late Dr. Ralph W. Leftwich.

Acknowledgements should also be made, in respect of the photographs, to the Oxford University Press, Mr. Emery Walker, Mr. Donald Macbeth (Artists Illustrators), Mr. A. P. Monger, Messrs. Vans and Crampton, Mr. R. Peach (Stratford-on-Avon), Messrs Annan (Glasgow), Messrs. Lambert, Weston & Son (Dover), and Mr. Jessop (Exmouth).

M. H. S.

LIST OF ILLUSTRATIONS

SHAKESPEARE'S PORTRAITURE:

The Title-Page : The Droeshout Print, the Stratford Bust, and Allied Portraits

I

THE mystery that veils so much in Shakespeare's genius, life, and work involves also some aspects of his Iconography. It is probable that of Shakespeare more portraits have been painted, drawn, engraved, and modelled, than of any other uncrowned king of men. Four thousand different possible ways of spelling his name have been classified and published;[1] the likenesses of him—in all methods of artistic expression—have been conceived on a proportionately lavish scale. The British Museum, it is true, according to its Catalogue, has only about 200 engraved portraits of the poet; the Grolier Club of New York, at its Tercentenary Exhibition in 1916, did better with about 450—including fifty each of the Bust and the Droeshout Plate. Many of us, no doubt, could have added scores to these, and I could have rounded them off with a collection of medals and token-coinage of Shakespeare, variants included, numbering well over 200.

And yet, of all these presentments only two portraits of the Poet can be regarded as authentic—as carrying the authority and the approval of his friends, relations, and fellow workers. That greatly simplifies the problem. Yet neither is directly a life-portrait;

[1] G. Wise, *The Autograph of William Shakespeare*, Philadelphia, 1869, 8vo.

B

and, as these two differ in certain minor, yet not
unimportant points, the way has been thrown open
to interminable controversy, to resistance—even to
violent hostility.   No doubt this is due to mis-
apprehension by persons indifferently versed in
matters of Iconography.   Yet there is a touch of
irony about it, that one or other of the only two
authentic portraits should be attacked, on occasion,
even by certain of the orthodox, with almost as much
virulence as misunderstanding, while other portraits, quite without claim to respect, are freely
accepted, meekly, abjectly, by the credulous.

The approximation of the two portraits, alike in
respect of authenticity, and, in the main, of identity
as regards actual bony structure—for herein they
support and complement one another—compels me
to take them together.   It is not possible to confine
oneself to Martin Droeshout's print on the title-page
of the First Folio.   And as the Stratford Bust, set
within its monument, came first in order of production, I take it first—as introduction to the Print by
Droeshout.   On this special occasion—seeing that
I am addressing myself to a body of students of
Shakespeare—I go more deeply into detail and into
exposition than might otherwise be desirable ; wherefore this Address becomes perhaps less of a Lecture
and more of a Demonstration.

The passion to know what manner of man Shakespeare really was gave rise, a generation or more ago,
to a demand [1] put forward on both sides of the
Atlantic that his deep grave should be opened and his
remains exhumed—in order that it might be decided
whether in the Bust or in the Print, or in both, we

---

[1] It was started, or re-started, by C. M. Ingleby, LL.D., V.-P.,
R.S.L., life trustee of Shakespeare's Birth-place and New Place, in
his tract entitled *Shakespeare's Bones*, 1883 (12 + 48 pp.).   There was
a forlorn attempt to revive the agitation four years ago.   1920

had the true likeness of the poet—(for bodies have been dug up from the damp soil of Stratford and after very many years have been found to have suffered little change).

A howl of protest was raised both in America and here at the proposed sacrilege. And yet the proposal was not by any means a novel one. In 1774, King Edward I—' Longshanks '—who had been buried 470 years, was exhumed by the Society of Antiquaries, and the King's waxed face and hands were found entire. Schiller's bones had been identified and collected from the bone-house in 1827, and the skull carried backwards and forwards and placed on exhibition. And nobody cried ' Shame ! ' In 1833 Raphael's tomb was opened, for identification, a cast taken of his skull and hands, and the skeleton publicly exhibited in a glass case. People tolerated even that. In 1813, during the regency of Prince George, the coffin of Charles I was opened, and the tragic head was found in a condition not very different from life, or rather, very recent death. At the same time that of Henry VIII—found battered—was opened, and a sketch was made of him. Some may remember George Cruikshank's bitter caricature on the double event which he used as a spiked bludgeon where-with to awaken the dormant conscience of the Prince Regent, not by reason of his reckless dissipation, but because he had permitted the tampering with the Royal Dead. Swedenborg's skull was taken and cast, in 1819, and that of Burns in 1834. And so on. But none dared, even if he would, face Shakespeare's Curse—that terribly deterrent piece of effective doggerel, which certainly was intended to play upon what the author of it knew to be the character and sentiment of the people. For he himself had had the opportunity of looking—with horror at the scandal which was there revealed—into the charnel-house

of Stratford Church. The superstructure of this
subterranean bone-house was razed in 1800, but the
underground portion of it, with all the bones through
long years pitched anyhow into it, still exists outside
the north wall of the church, and within a yard or
two of Shakespeare's monument.

No man has dared to 'digg' the Poet's 'dvst'.
In order to circumvent the Curse,—

—AND CVRST BE *HE* Y^T MOVES MY BONES—

it was ingeniously suggested that *women* should
undertake the operation. But the proposal happily
came to nothing, whether or not women could have
been found who would risk the awful malediction
and damnation of a Shakespeare's Curse.

Chronologically, then, the first place is here taken
by the monument and its effigy erected in the north
wall of the chancel—by way of introduction to Droeshout of the Folios.

Of course, the design of a bust, really a half-length
statue, set in its niche—especially in the case of a
writing-man at his occupation—was in its way almost
a hackneyed form of sepulchral monument—almost a
cliché. For example, you will remember the monument of the chronicler, John Stow (Plate 1), set up by
his widow in St. Andrew Undershaft in the City, in
1605, from twelve to seventeen years before Shakespeare's was erected in Stratford-upon-Avon. We
see him writing. Nearly one hundred years before,
that of Dean Colet of St. Paul's—seated in a niche
with his hands before him on a book—was erected in
Old St. Paul's ; while there, also, was the not
dissimilar monument of Alexander Nowell, Dean
forty years later, done in 1601, with the hands upon
just such a cushion before him ; and others are to
be found about the country, in Canterbury Cathedral

PLATE 1

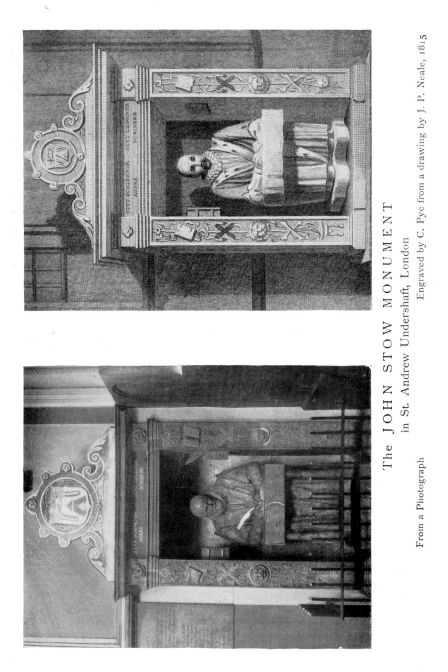

The JOHN STOW MONUMENT
in St. Andrew Undershaft, London

From a Photograph

Engraved by C. Pye from a drawing by J. P. Neale, 1815

PLATE 2

The CHANDOS PORTRAIT
In the National Portrait Gallery
(Copyright of Emery Walker)

The CHANDOS PORTRAIT
as engraved by Antonio Locatelli, 1822

PLATE 3

The Original Painting by JANSSEN
(By permission of the late Lady Helen Guendolen Ramsden
and the late Sir John Ramsden)
Copyright strictly reserved.

The JANSSEN PORTRAIT
as engraved by R. Dunkarton, 1811

PLATE 4

The FELTON PORTRAIT

As it is

As engraved by T. Trotter, 1794
imitating the Droeshout Print
by order of W. Richardson

and elsewhere. They are all based on much earlier examples of analogous portraiture, such for example as Botticelli's painting, of 1480, in the Uffizi Gallery at Florence, showing St. Augustine seated in a niche, writing, quill in hand (very like the Stow monument); and the portrait of Bishop Stokesley, at Windsor, wrongly attributed to Holbein, but painted before 1533; and numerous others that might be quoted.

In view of the argument which I am about to develop, I ask you to observe Stow's head—and then the head which the engraver Pye, in collusion with the draughtsman Neale, made of it only 100 years ago—to say nothing of the ermine, gratuitously thrown in. And yet these artists were in London and could easily have secured correctness had they wished. It illustrates engravers' disloyal indifference to accuracy, until the advent of photography brought truth along with it, and swept the fraudulent draughtsman and engraver from the field.

There is interest in one or two more apposite examples. Take the Chandos portrait (Plate 2) and note well this apparently swarthy alien. And then the famous engraver Locatelli's rendering of the picture—a rather startling caricature. *Locatelli drew it, genine engraver*

Or take the beautiful original Cornelis Janssen painting called 'of Shakespeare', belonging to the Ramsden family (Plate 3), and compare with it Dunkarton's engraved representation of it, wherein the resemblance lies only in the collar.

And yet again; the high-shouldered Felton portrait (Plate 4)—which belonged to the Baroness Burdett-Coutts—at the recent sale so amusingly paid for in the sum of £1,522 for America. Trotter's engraving audaciously sets it on the Droeshout low shoulders and doubleted body of the Droeshout print.

Is not all this sufficient proof that publishers and engravers, down to the early nineteenth century, cared nothing for truth of rendering, unless circumstances compelled ?

As with all of these, so with the Stratford Monument and Bust.

After 1616, but not later than 1622, the Stratford Monument (Plate 5), of a design kindred to those already mentioned, was erected—it is assumed, but without any positive evidence—to the order of Shakespeare's son-in-law, Dr. John Hall.   In any case, it must have had the approval of Mistress Shakespeare and her family, and have received and withstood the criticism of Shakespeare's friends and associates.   According to Sir William Dugdale it was the work of Garratt Janssen or Johnson, the Anglo-Flemish tomb-maker of Southwark, whose father had been resident in London since 1567.

In style it is a work of the pure Jacobean Renaissance and manifestly of the time.   It has beauty of design, and is characteristic alike in detail and proportion—an harmonious and compact whole.

The mantling about the shield is contemporary in style, and the whole exactly what we are accustomed to find from the tomb-makers of the period, among whom Nicholas Stone, working in conjunction with Bernard Janssen—probably a kinsman of Garratt—is a noteworthy example.   The same details reappear constantly in their work, both Bernard's and Garratt's, in a whole series of tombs and monuments, and we need go no farther than to the Charterhouse and look there at the tomb of the pious founder, Thomas Sutton, to recognize that such details, both architectural and sculptural, were, as it were, stereotyped in the work of these leaders of their craft—stock designs used by the three men.

A noteworthy feature is the cherub-like boys

PLATE 5

The SHAKESPEARE MONUMENT
Holy Trinity Church, Stratford-on-Avon

PLATE 6

The STRATFORD MONUMENT
(Seventeenth-Century Work)

The Upper Section showing the Boys with their Attributes

(Plate 6), who sit up aloft. It is important to note that these little figures, unfinished at the back, are carved *in one piece with the little mounds* on which they sit—the one on the left holds a spade, the other an inverted, extinguished torch, one hand resting upon a skull—intended to represent Labour and Rest—not symbols of mortality, as one would suppose. This ancient piece of classic symbolism is frequently to be seen in the work of Stone and others. These figures, which I have examined closely on the several occasions on which I have been permitted to go up and take measurements of the work in its many details, are quite manifestly early seventeenth-century work ; they not only bear the impress of the sentiment of the time, but their surface and texture bring further witness. They are not attached to the monument, but are movable. The material of which the monument is composed is white marble, with black touchstone inlaid in slabs, and beneath there is the support of the usual alabaster brackets—that is to say, the two outside brackets are of alabaster, the middle one, replacing an original now lost, is badly painted in imitation of alabaster. It was, of course, to this monument that the very minor poet, Leonard Digges, alluded when to the First Folio he contributed his awkward but very sincere and honest verses of homage comprised in the oft-quoted lines beginning :

Shake-speare, *at length thy pious fellowes giue*
The world thy Workes : thy Workes, by which, out-liue
Thy Tombe, thy name must : when that stone is rent,
And Time dissolues thy Stratford *Moniment,*
Here we aliue shall view thee still. This Booke,
When Brasse and Marble fade, shall make thee looke
Fresh to all Ages : when Posteritie
Shall loath what 's new, thinke all is prodegie
That is not Shake-speares.

This sentiment was not infrequently expressed in epitaphs on men of letters. For example, the epitaph on Drayton's tomb in Westminster Abbey (attributed alike to Quarles and Ben Jonson) invokes the ' pious marble ' of his monument :

> And when thy ruins shall disclaim
> To be the treasure of his name,—
> His name that cannot fade, shall be
> An everlasting monument to thee.

In looking at the bust, we must bear in mind that the large majority of casts which we find about are not casts from the original at all—not even the one in the National Portrait Gallery—although at first glance they look very like it—but from copies which depart more or less gravely from Janssen's work ; and that many of the ' Engravings from the Bust ' are done from these inaccurate copies. Criticisms levelled at the bust have been frequently based upon examination of these misleading casts. Here then, is the portrait of Shakespeare given us by his family, and approved necessarily by Mistress Shakespeare (who lived just long enough to see the First Folio itself) and by the poet's friends and fellow-townsmen who knew him well. This bust, like the figure of Shakespeare's friend, John Combe, who lies close by (the tomb having been made also by Garratt Janssen), is of limestone from the neighbourhood of Stroud—a soft stone in common use when the sculpture was to be coloured. It is, therefore, intentionally lacking in modelling, because the colour would be left to do its work—the eyebrows so lightly chiselled that they hardly suggest the hair ; and in the open mouth the teeth without divisions, in one band, which is painted white. For if such a bust were fully modelled, and then painted, and the division of the teeth clearly marked, it would look more like a waxwork, and lose that breadth and gravely monumental aspect of treatment which are proper to a sepulchral work.

No one with a close and familiar understanding of sculpture will say that it is eighteenth-century work, except as regards some unimportant repairs hardly to be identified. It not only corresponds exactly with the treatment of the features in the head of Combe, it reveals not only the same sculptor's hand—but it shows the same costume. It has generally been asserted by the technical expert that it was modelled direct from a mask, taken from the subject. Chantrey (who was as great an admirer of the bust as were Malone, Landor, Washington Irving, Matthew Arnold,[1] and Mr. Arthur Benson of to-day) believed it to be from a death-mask, for the reason that the raised lip shows a contraction of muscle which suggests the *rigor mortis*—as if any sculptor, however unskilful, would be fool enough deliberately to introduce into a bust, purporting to represent a living, and obviously a robust and humorous-minded man, a corpse's rigidity! The fact is that the muscle may be contracted quite as much in life under the unpleasant experience of a mask being taken—when warm wax or cold wet plaster is poured over the face, with breathing-straws thrust into the nostrils, and perhaps a breathing-tube between the lips. This was also the opinion of Sir Thomas Brock, who took life-masks in his day as well as death-masks. The curious, and at first sight stupid, aspect of the bust arises from more than one fact. In the first place, the eyes and nose, inter-relatively, and proportionately, are too small for the face. From close and careful examination I maintain that there is no foundation for the suggestion, frequently

[1] . . . Thou smilest and art still,
    Out-topping knowledge.

C

printed, that from the nose a piece had at some time been broken off, and repaired, to make the best of a bad job, by carving it down to a smaller scale. But even were this the case, the eyes would still be too close together. There is not the slightest evidence of breakage, or of recarving of the nose or nostrils : on the contrary, the evidence of the bust is against it. The open lids of the eyes have been modelled coarsely—eyes are closed when a mask is taken, and they have to be modelled up afterwards —the lips are straight and open, indicating, according to the taste of some, ' the agony of death ', and according to that of others, ' the hilarity of a mighty humorist ' : it all depends on whether they are adherents of the death-mask-theory or of the life-mask-theory, according as their fancy dictates.

The upper lip which has puzzled so many by its appearance of inordinate depth—comparable, it was said, to that of Liston and Walter Scott—is in fact *not long at all*. It is three-quarters of an inch full and seven-eighths bare from the septum of the nose to the lip—practically the length of my own upper lip. This so amazed me when I was transcribing my notes at the hotel that I went back to the church, re-mounted the scaffolding, and took the measurement afresh ; but with the same result. The fact remained a puzzling one until a thought struck me. Returned to the hotel I procured a cork, and having burned it, I corked upon my lip just such a moustache as that on the Stratford bust—in style a fashion said to be not uncommon though by no means general at the time—(as in the portrait of Shakespeare's contemporary, Maurice Prince of Orange, Plate 7). I was very careful to leave the proper space of bare flesh between the nose and the moustache and again above the lip itself (*à la* Richard Baxter, 1615), and I was startled—not to say

PLATE 7

MAURICE PRINCE OF ORANGE, 1567–1625
To illustrate the fashion of wearing the moustache
As in the Shakespeare Effigy

PLATE 9

The STRATFORD MONUMENT
The Effigy

proud—to find my own lip suddenly lengthened into a true Shakespearian feature. Any clean-shaven man who will make the experiment will bear out what I say.

As to the proportions of Shakespeare's features, I have scribbled here a sketch from the ' Remarks ' of Rumsey Forster of 1849 (Plate 8). We take the Droeshout Engraving on the left, the Bust on the right, and the Chandos painting in the middle, with horizontal lines passing across the top of the cranium and through the eyes of each ; and below the

RELATIVE PROPORTIONS OF THE THREE HEADS
DROESHOUT—CHANDOS—STRATFORD EFFIGY
(From *Rumsey Forster, 1849*)

nose, and through the mouth, of the Chandos. We find that the nose, in the Bust, is relatively as long as that of the Chandos but is longer in the Droeshout ; while the mouths of the Bust and Print are on the same horizontal. The common similarity is greater than one would have supposed.

The costume is that worn by a serious-minded gentleman of the day—to be found in innumerable portraits—a sleeveless gown over a doublet (Plate 9) ; the head—that of a robust orator, supposed to be declaiming what he has just written—is made staring by the unskilful and vulgar brush by which the exaggerated pupils of the eyes have been drawn and coloured ; and the stupidly hard, coarsely-shaped, half-moon eyebrows—more like George Robey's than anybody else's—have been accentuated and set too high on the frontal bone. During the period when the bust was painted white by Malone's influence no one complained of its wooden appearance and vapid expression. But even then such chisel-work as there is, was concealed by the paint from view. The poor journeyman-work of the repainting of the bust had destroyed what attractiveness Janssen had put into his half-length statue. And yet, lacking as the work is in artistic merit, it has just sufficient marks of facial individuality to prevent it from being generalized in the manner common enough in earlier sepulchral sculpture. It is not too life-like or intimate ; and while suggesting resemblance, it makes no pretence of giving the smaller accidents of the life, which, however permissible in ordinary portrait-busts and statues, are gravely out of place on tombs and in monuments. That is why that wonderfully, magically life-like seated statue of Wilberforce, by Samuel Joseph, R.S.A., in Westminster Abbey, makes us marvel at the absolute vitality of the marble ; we may look, almost expectant that this noble figure may be just going to sneeze—but never are we made to think of the statue as a solemn sepulchral tribute to a great philanthropist passed away set up in the National Valhalla. The *bravura* has destroyed the solemnity. Better for the occasion is the stiff simplicity of Shakespeare's bust in Holy Trinity Church at Stratford.

It has actually been claimed by the adherents of the hopelessly unauthentic and discredited Kesselstadt Death-Mask, that that object was the original authority on which the bust was based, as some of the measurements correspond. Certain of the linear measurements agree, no doubt, as measurements of men's heads will sometimes correspond by chance ; but measurements may tally as those of a circle and

The Death-Mask was purchased in England by count Franz Kesselstadt about the end of the 18th century.

an oval may tally, but without correspondence in the outward forms ; and while in the death-mask the forehead recedes, in the bust it tends towards the perpendicular—that is to say, the bony structure differs fundamentally—and as chief features also differ, radically, in shape and form and inter-relation, it is impossible, on that ground alone, to admit connexion.

In accordance with the usual practice, then, the Stratford Bust was coloured—indeed, the Flemings, to whom we owe so much of our art, from the middle of the fifteenth century onwards, generally refused to accept sculpture of the kind without colour. Examples of this class abound throughout England. I need not remind you that Shakespeare himself identified statuary with colour, as in the *Winter's Tale* (v. iii—1610)—when Paulina would restrain the ardour of King Leontes and his daughter Perdita before what they think to be the statue of Queen Hermione—and they would kiss it. Paulina cries

> ' O Patience !
> The Statue is but newly fix'd, the colour 's
> Not dry . . . .
> . . . . . Good my Lord, forbear :
> The ruddiness upon her lip is wet ;
> You'll mar it if you kiss it, stain your own
> With oily painting.'

So, too, Ben Jonson in *The Magnetic Lady* (v. 5) produced at the Blackfriars Theatre twenty-two years later. He scoffs at the practice :

Rut says :
> ' I'd have her statue cut now in white marble.'

Sir Moth Interest replies :
> ' And have it painted in most orient colours '—

To which Rut rejoins :
> ' That 's right ! All city statues must be painted ;
> Else they'll be worth nought in their subtle judgments.'

The painted face of the bust shows a glow of health usually to be seen only in sculptured effigies. The hair and beard are auburn; the doublet scarlet; the gown black; the falling-band white; the cushion green above and crimson below; the cord and tassels gilt. The eyes are hazel gone dark. The eyes are always the most untrustworthy part in an old portrait, for two reasons : in the first place, from the point of view of colour, because being the thinnest in pigment, in order to preserve the effect of limpidity, the eyes are liable to change—and, in the second, when a picture is cleaned, the eyes often disappear first along with the varnish removed, and have to be reinstated, frequently without proper matching by the careless restorer who has failed to make a note of the true colour before beginning his work.

Within recent years the misdirected critical spirit which is afoot has attempted to upset the authenticity of the bust and monument as we know them, on the slender basis, firstly, of the absurd plate in Dugdale's *Antiquities of Warwickshire*, and the irresponsible imitations of it ; and secondly, of certain repairs made in 1748 ; and the error has been so widely repeated and seized upon, both by the unwary and by the Shakespeare-haters that I must ask to be allowed a moment or two in which to remove the misconception.

In 1656 Sir William Dugdale published his great *Warwickshire* which was declared to be his masterpiece (up to that time) and to stand at the head of all our county histories ; and Dr. Whitaker reminded his readers that Dugdale's 'scrupulous accuracy ranked as legal evidence'.

Personally, on many points on which I have consulted Dugdale, both text and illustrations—I have found him inaccurate on simple matters of fact.

*
See picture
opp p. 257
Shakespeare
Anthony Burgess
Knopf.
New York 1970

Not only does he assert that Combe's monument, close by, is of alabaster whereas it is of sandstone, but, among other things, he transcribes inaccurately as to spelling the inscriptions on Shakespeare's monument and gravestone, and on the gravestones of the Shakespeare family in the chancel of the church.

?

Dr. William Thomas edited the second edition of the *Warwickshire* in 1730, and complained that he found to his ' great surprise (when his own work was finished) that the account which Sir William Dugdale had given [of certain parishes] was very imperfect '—that a register was confused, another wholly omitted, others reversed, also epitaphs and coats-of-arms in churches passed over ; but he excuses Dugdale by saying *that they were done by persons he hired* ' who took them down as they pleased themselves to spare their own pains '. That is to say, Dugdale was at the mercy of his assistants. And in 1730 a vitriolic book of 250 pages was published by Charles Hornby violently attacking Dugdale's very numerous mistakes in his *Baronage of England* (1675–6, 3 volumes).

1670 – 1738 DNB.

Could it well have been otherwise ? The amazingly industrious Dugdale was the busiest of writers and compilers, and great works—monumental works— stiff with facts, figures, lists, and so forth, came from him in quick succession. In 1656, with the help of Sir Symon Archer, appeared his *Antiquities of Warwickshire* with 812 folio pages. In 1655—a year before—had appeared the first volume of his tremendous *Monasticon Anglicanum* with 1,150 folio pages— the book which was accepted as ' circumstantial evidence in the Courts '. Only two years later was published his great *History of St. Paul's Cathedral* [with its ludicrous discrepancies, as to its measurements, between himself and his illustrator Hollar [1]]—

[1] ' . . . Dugdale, with a minute and apparent exactness, states the

Sir Symon Archer : (1581 – 1662) antiquary ; knighted in 1624 ; Sheriff of Warwickshire 1628 MP 1640 He amassed much of the material used in Dugdales ' History of Warwickshire ' and other valuable antiquarian information – DNB.

all these works with many plates—and in 1662 another important work, *History of Imbanking and Drainage*, followed four years afterwards by *Origines Juridiciales*, and another great folio. Rarely, if ever, has such a series of works—packed with records and details, facts, dates, names, armorial shields, inscriptions, and the like—the result of wide and deep research and amazing industry—fallen from one pen, or one editorship, in the course of ten years. The *Monasticon* is full of engraved plates, most of them of cathedrals and churches, many grotesquely false, as for example, those in which Exeter and York Cathedrals are shown with semi-circular-headed windows and doors instead of Gothic, proportions incorrect, and kindred misrepresentations in others. Are we to take those plates as evidence that the Cathedrals have been endowed with a different order of architecture since the plates were published?

The fact is that Dugdale, who concentrated his attention mainly on armorial bearings and monuments and cared little for portrait-busts and architecture, was victimized both by his helpers and his artists, at the head of whom was Hollar, with his assistants Gaywood, Daniel King (whom Hollar himself called ' an ignorant silly knave '), Dudley, Carter, and several more. Hollar, whom Dugdale invited to England on a second visit in 1652, has been undeservedly vaunted, as much as Dugdale, for his invariable fidelity and accuracy. Infallibility was claimed for him. Walpole said ' he had no rival in point of truth to nature and art ', and Gilpin alluded to ' his great truth ' and ' exact reproduction'.

length at 690 feet, and this measurement has been repeated by every subsequent writer to the present day. It is remarkable that this does not correspond with the plan, laid out to scale, which accompanies Dugdale's description.' (William Longman, *A History of the Three Cathedrals dedicated to St. Paul in London*. . . . London, 1873 (p. 29).)

But truthful as he was in still-life subjects and certain topographical plates, Hollar was as fallible as his employer, and as hard-worked.[1]   As diligent as Dugdale, he was the busiest of artists. He is credited with 2,400 plates (many large and elaborate), or forty-eight plates a year—about one a week, for fifty years ; he was so busy that he cared not much more for troublesome accuracy than others of his time and class—who cared next to nothing. In 1644 the *Mercurius Civicus* (the first English illustrated paper), gave a portrait in four successive weekly numbers of Prince Maurice, Prince Rupert, the Marquess of Newcastle, and Sir Thomas Fairfax—and it was the same portrait each time, and nothing changed but the name ; so that ' near enough ' was the motto of the time.[2] For the plates to this *Monasticon* and other works, the artists would make rough sketches and written notes, or use another man's, and, returned to London—on such occasions as they had left it—work all up together at home as best they could—from memory sometimes, as there is ample evidence—confusing parts, and even monuments and Orders of architecture. They could not be expected to be more accurate than Dugdale himself.

Now Hollar was the chief engraver of the *War-wickshire* ; and as the Shakespeare monument we

[1] ' . . . It must be stated, in justification of the bold attempt to represent [Old] St. Paul's more correctly than was done by Hollar, who actually saw the building, that Hollar's plates are full of evident inaccuracies. One plate contradicts another, and, indeed, scarcely two of them agree, as will be seen by the appendix to this chapter.' William Longman, *op. cit.*, pp. 37–40. Then follows a list, a page and a half long, of Hollar's obvious blunders—contradictions of himself, of established facts, and of Dugdale's statements.

[2] So, too, in William Jaggard's small folio : *A View of all the Right Honourable Lord Mayors of this Honourable Citty of London* (1601), of which the only recorded copy was sold in the Britwell Court Library sale of the 2nd of April, 1924, ' eleven woodcut portraits alone are used for the forty-five Lord Mayors, most of them occurring several times.'

D

know does not agree with the plate in Dugdale, it has been innocently assumed and asserted as fact by persons unfamiliar with the ways of the earlier engravers, that the Stratford monument as we know it, and as it is here before us, is another, a different, monument and not the original—inasmuch as the proportions, as well as the details, are wholly different, and the bust presents no similarity whatever. This belief pathetically recalls the peasant's faith in the printed word because it is ' in the papers '.

Very well. Let me produce some further evidence. Most of us know the statue of Charles I by Hubert Le Sueur, of 1633, looking towards Whitehall (Plate 10), with its splendid contemporary base (wrongly attributed to Grinling Gibbons—it was carved by Joshua Marshall). The king holds his baton in his right hand, and the horse, his head turned aside, holds up his *right* fore-leg. Now, in Hollar's engraving of it the pedestal is unrecognizable ; the King still holds his baton in his right hand, but the horse, with his head straight forward, holds up his *left* fore-leg instead of the right. Therefore, according to modern reasoning this whole monument must be new ; the pedestal as well—for this, without decoration, is only half the height, though in plan it is fairly correct. It is clearly meant for the pedestal. As it happens, however, certain contemporaries of Hollar show the monument correctly. But Dugdale was a Warwickshire man, and had great pride in Shakespeare (as his book shows), so that, it is suggested, he would take pains to have the monument and effigy correctly drawn—more especially, we are told, as all the monuments in Stratford Church except Shakespeare's are rendered with accuracy. As a matter of fact, only two others in the church were engraved, both of them faultily—one

PLATE 10

STATUE OF KING CHARLES I
at Charing Cross

As it is

As engraved by Hollar

PLATE 11

AS IT IS

(From a photograph)

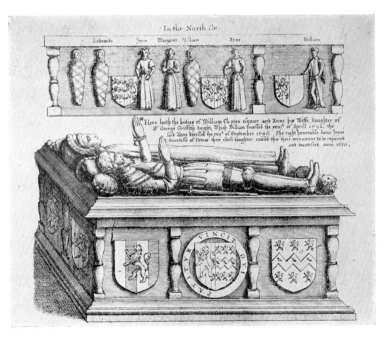

AS ENGRAVED IN DUGDALE'S *Antiquities of Warwickshire*, 1656

The CLOPTON MONUMENT

In Holy Trinity Church, Stratford-on-Avon

PLATE 12

The CAREW MONUMENT
Holy Trinity Church, Stratford-on-Avon

As it is
From a Photograph

As engraved in Dugdale's
Antiquities of Warwickshire, 1656

of them grotesquely so. The first of these is the Clopton monument (Plate 11). You see the attitudes of the small figures on the frieze representing Clopton's children, and below the figure of the knight beside his wife, his head resting on his helmet, the crest of which is away from us, and the opening towards us. In the Dugdale plate the helmet is reversed, although it is carved out of one piece of alabaster with the figure ; and the gauntlet beside the knight's leg, into which the scabbard disappears, is omitted altogether. There are other striking differences. It is clear that the sketches taken in Stratford were insufficient to provide for a correct plate to be engraved later on in London, supposing that accuracy was sincerely desired.

Far more reckless are the errors to be found in the Carew monument (Plate 12). Here the lady lies on the outside, the husband inside. We note the angels standing upon the projecting cornices at the sides ; the horizontal shape of all the three panels bearing inscriptions and of the frieze at the bottom—powder-barrels to the left ; and to the right, cannon pointing to the *right*—in allusion to Carew being Master of Ordnance.

But in Dugdale's plate the proportion is utterly different. Elongated pinnacles (exactly such as we see in the monument of Alexander Nowell in Dugdale's *St. Paul's Cathedral*, also engraved under the direction of Hollar) take the place of the figures ; the arms at the top are much reduced in size ; the artist has left himself room for only two panels and so omits the third. He reverses the positions of the figures. He puts the knight *outside*, his body directed the other way ; and in the frieze, while he retains the powder-barrels in their proper position, he points the cannon the other way round—to the left ; and every other single detail, when examined carefully, is seen to differ from the original. It all shows lack of memory as to objects although a vague idea of facts is untidily retained.

We find equal inaccuracy in the equally 'impeccable' Vertue whose artistic honesty Walpole so warmly extols to the disadvantage of the Dutchman, Houbraken—Vertue's collaborator in Birch's *Heads of Illustrious Persons* (1747), and as an engraver vastly his superior. Yet the enemies of the Shakespeare monument have not presumed to claim these Clopton and Carew monuments also as modern substitutions. They slur the facts over, and fix only upon the Dugdale engraving, which most probably was from the graver of Gaywood, already named as one of the ill-paid hacks employed by the publishers to engrave on brass or copper plates from sketches supplied to them.

Let us take the page in Dugdale of 1656 which shows the Clopton monument above, and Shakespeare's below, as first published to the world (Plate 13). We see at once the lamentable proportions of the monument as here misrepresented, while the style inclines to Baroque—a style some twenty or thirty years later than Shakespeare's death, but already sprung into existence when the *Warwickshire* was published. It therefore gives itself the lie. We see the poor design of the shield and mantling, the ridiculous boys cut off their mounds and perched insecurely on the edge of the cornice, little architectural in sentiment—the one holding aloft a spade, and the other an hour-glass, as shown, totally unsculptural in effect. The arch is of a different form, perhaps to allow the wide space necessary for the unauthentic, stuck-out elbows of the figure. The portrait is no portrait at all : it shows us a sickly, decrepit old gentleman, with a falling moustache, much more than fifty-two years old. Had Shake-

Design possibly taken from Jansen prior to execution for tomb of John Shakespeare 1601 - See page 4 bottom description of tomb for Alexander Nowell in Old St. Pauls in 1601 - DNB gives 1602

PLATE 13

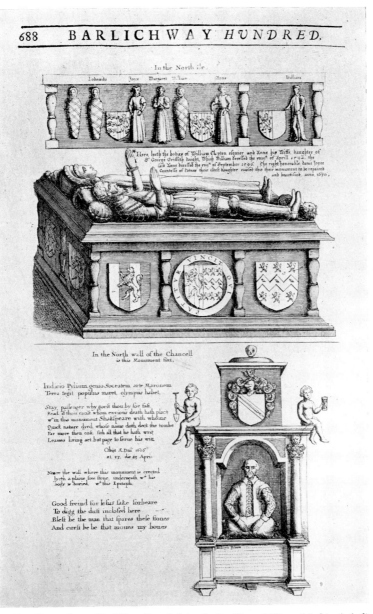

The Page from Sir Wm. Dugdale's *Antiquities of Warwickshire* (1656) showing, below, the engraving (altered from his original sketch) purporting to represent the SHAKESPEARE MONUMENT in Holy Trinity Church, Stratford-on-Avon ; and, above, the CLOPTON MONUMENT

PLATE 14

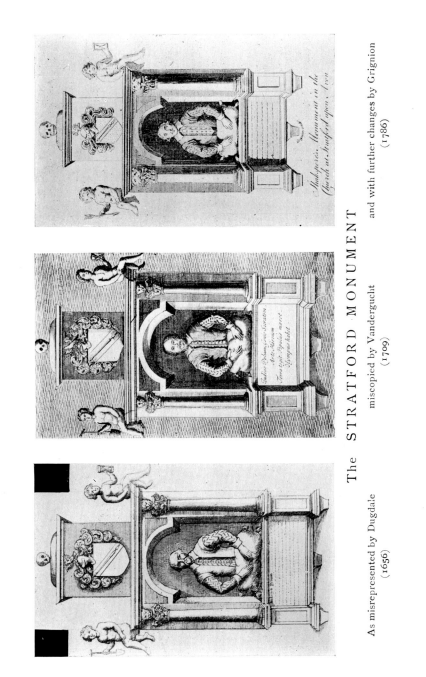

As misrepresented by Dugdale
(1656)

The STRATFORD MONUMENT

miscopied by Vandergucht
(1709)

and with further changes by Grignion
(1786)

speare been really such in his last illness would the London sculptor have so rendered him? Do sculptors, in their monuments, represent the great departed in their dying state, pressing pillows to their stomachs? Yet both hands are here upon a cushion which, for no reason, except perhaps abdominal pains, is hugged against what dancing-masters euphemistically term the 'lower chest', and the whole is supported not by brackets but by three small feet, standing upon the ground.[1] Other hack engravers followed this wretched performance, of course for other publishers, each one copying the last, instead of contradicting it by taking the trouble, and incurring the expense, of the journey to Stratford to sketch for themselves; wherefore their imitations, in spite of differences of their own, made for the purpose of avoiding charges of plagiarism (believing their 'original' to be correct)—have actually been accepted as confirmatory evidence by those unskilled in the ways of hack engravers and adventurer-publishers of Dugdale's day.

See below

So the frontispiece to one volume of Rowe's edition of Shakespeare, which Tonson published in 1709, gives us Vandergucht's version, which is a fairly favourable copy of Dugdale, except for the false panel and inscription; it is, in fact, absolutely worthless (Plate 14).

In 1786 Charles Grignion stole Vandergucht's design for Dr. Johnson's and Steevens's edition, taking care to introduce 'originality' by altering the spade into an arrow, and bringing in the elbows and narrowing the arch. Grignion, a native of London, had a great reputation, and—the friend and engraver

---

[1] It is the fact that the original drawing for this engraving is extant and in the possession of a lineal descendant of Dugdale, and that the plate departs in details from the sketch. Why? One of them, obviously, must be wrong. In truth, both are libels on the original.

of Hogarth—maintained his position for half a century as the chief engraver for the booksellers, by whom he was kept closely to his copper-plates, at that time the principal method of good illustration.

Then comes the so-called scrupulous Vertue, who could be as inaccurate as the rest, and who coolly places the head of the Chandos portrait—the popular portrait of the day—on the shoulders of the effigy ! (Plate 15)—just as he complacently engraved the Welbeck miniature (of a totally different person) and represented it to be Shakespeare.   But the deadly thing is that this engraving, which was done for Tonson in 1723—or twenty-five years *before* the alleged ' radical reconstruction ' of the monument, which is pretended to have occurred in 1748— presents that monument to us pretty well *exactly as it is to-day*—all except the head ! The mantling, the architectural proportions, the figure with its hands ready to write upon a cushion, the seated cherubs, and the brackets, are all the same— brackets, be it observed, instead of feet, just as to-day—except only that, with poetic licence and incorrigible perversity, he daintily places impossible burning tapers in the boys' hands, as more likely than arrow and hour-glass ; and (as you may see) no leopards' heads are introduced on either side of the frieze.   But what else can we expect, seeing that Vertue paid his first visit to Stratford in 1737—that is to say, twelve years after he had made a ' copy ' of the monument on which he had never set eyes— like the copyists of Dugdale's plate ?

Thus the game was carried on—and five years later, in 1728, for Pope's edition, Fourdrinier just copied Vertue, maintaining the architectural character of the present monument.   This, at least, is a tribute to its genuineness, for, as it is now, such you see it obviously was in 1723 ; and as in 1723,

Could Vertue have been hired to design the alteration of the monument and that his visit in 1737 was the check up on the alteration

PLATE 15

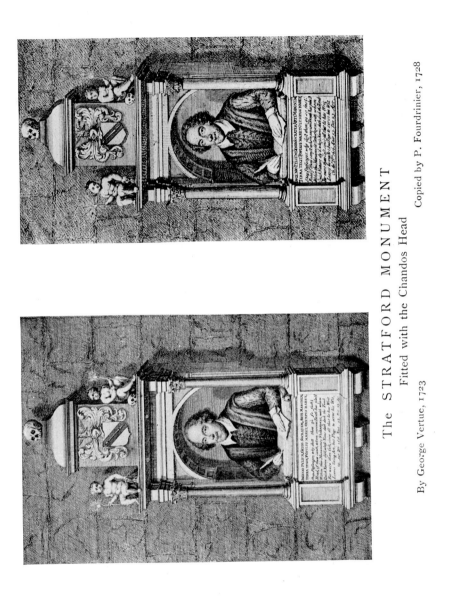

The STRATFORD MONUMENT
Fitted with the Chandos Head

By George Vertue, 1723

Copied by P. Fourdrinier, 1728

so in 1620. As to the authenticity of the effigy itself, which ignorant critics pretend to be a modern one, I am about to offer final evidence.

The grounds for the attack on the monument are these. In 1649—nearly thirty years after it was erected—the bust was, as it was called, ' re-beautified ', that is to say, repainted in its colours, for the church was damp, and the painted figure and its shrine had suffered. In 1746, nearly 100 years later, it was said to have fallen in such a state of (superficial) decay that John Ward, grandfather of Mrs. Siddons, and head of a company of strolling players, gave a performance of *Othello* at Stratford, and devoted the proceeds to ' repairing and beautifying ' the monument. This has been curiously interpreted —with the treacherous backing of the Dugdale plate and the copies of it—as having been radically a renovation to the extent of a virtual substitution, in order to justify Dugdale's enormity—although to this day, the Combe monument hard by, erected at the same time, has never had to be touched, and is in a sound condition, except that a number of the little sculptured rosettes have fallen from the coffered arched roof. The Clopton monument also has been ' repaired and re-beautified ' ; yet no one claims or imagines that it has been reconstructed.

John Hall, a painter, was employed for the renovation ; but, when we look into the history of that renovation, naïvely put forward by the main supporters of the new theory, and accepted by the blind followers of it, we find that the amount raised from the *Othello* performance was no more than £12 10*s*., and that the *repairs* which were effected after two years of wrangling, are supposed to have resulted in this fine new marble monument and carved stone bust for that paltry sum ! In 1793 Malone, with the permission of the vicar, Mr. Davenport, had the bust painted white—not ' whitewashed ' as some writers have affirmed. In 1861 the white-lead paint was removed with solvents by Simon Collins, and the damaged paint underneath boldly and summarily restored in its proper colours, though in too high a key. The first joint of the finger was broken off, and the second fractured, in 1748, and the lead pen had disappeared ; but Fairholt declared that no other damage existed. New fingers were said to be supplied by William Roberts, of Oxford, in 1790.

Now, in the Whitechapel Shakespearian and Theatrical Exhibition of 1910, a little picture was lent by the late Earl of Warwick, *showing the monument practically as it is to-day* (Plate 16). The painting is 19 inches high by 13 wide. I obtained permission to photograph it, and I found, pasted on the back, a label with the following inscription signed by Halliwell-Phillipps : ' This old painting of the monumental effigy of Shakespeare is of great curiosity, being the one painted by Hall *before he re-coloured the bust in* 1748. The letters proving this are in the possession of Richard Greene, Esq., F.S.A., who presented them some years ago to *Fraser's Magazine*. I purchased the picture of Mr. Greene, who is the lineal descendant of the Rev. Joseph Greene of Stratford, the owner of the painting of about 1770. J. O. Halliwell ' —(that is to say, Halliwell-Phillipps). I think we can leave the matter here ; but it may be added that it is pretended that the gown, not being visible in the Dugdale print, has been ' added ' to the bust—as if you could add a mantle to a completed piece of sculpture when the whole, mantle and figure too, was carved from a single block ! Every sculptor, and every one else with any knowledge of the arts, shrugs his shoulders at the suggestion.

There is an interesting question which might be

Halliwell suspected as did Malone that the gown was a point of argument against the effigy

PLATE 16

The STRATFORD MONUMENT
Painted by John Hall, before 1748—the date
of its misalleged reconstruction

By permission of the late Earl of Warwick

discussed as to whether the monument has ever
been removed from an earlier position to that it
now occupies. There is solid evidence in support of
this, but it is foreign to our purpose at the moment.

II

Martin, or *Marten*, *Droeshout*, whose immortal
piece of inferior engraving we are now to consider,
was only twenty-two years old when his plate was

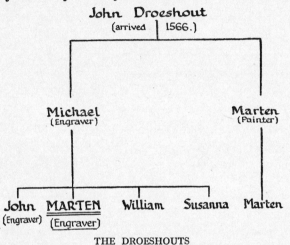

THE DROESHOUTS

published—and probably less by a year or so when
he engraved it. He was one of a family of engravers,
as may be seen in the little genealogical ' tree '
above, based mainly on Dr. Lionel Cust's re-
searches among the records of the Dutch Church
at Austin Friars.

John Droeshout, a Fleming, who had arrived in
London from Brussels in 1566, was a joiner and
painter. His elder son, Michael, an engraver, was
the father of John, MARTIN (*our* Martin)—both of
them second-rate artist-craftsmen—and of two other
children, who do not concern us. How young

E

Droeshout came to be chosen to engrave the portrait for the great volume can only be guessed : his family, and the family of the master-mason, Garratt Johnson the younger, who had lately completed Shakespeare's monument at Stratford—were members of the same church and allied to the same colony at Blackfriars. The recommendation and introduction, therefore, were natural enough.

The boy got the commission. What he made of it has provided material for unfavourable comment by most modern critics. The portrait would hardly justify Aubrey's statement that Shakespeare ' was a handsome well-shap't man ', yet the technique of it shows that Martin could engrave a sweet line— that he had a pleasing command of the graver.

We must keep the bust, or effigy, in mind while we turn to Martin Droeshout's Print—which truly, being a portrait of Shakespeare when a much younger man than him of the bust, should have taken precedence. The bust, of course, professes to show us what the Poet looked like when he had put on flesh and bobbed his hair ; yet in spite of the fact that the adipose tissue has rounded forms and filled up hollows, broadened masses and generally increased dimensions—we recognize that the perpendicular forehead and the shape of the skull are very much the same in both ; and we further observe that whereas the Droeshout Print shows us chiefly the width of the forehead *across the temples*, the full-face of the bust gives the shape of the head further back, across *where the ears are set on*. The result, by comparison, is a piece of facial rotundity—surely far less ethereal even than what Mr. J. C. Squire calls ' the pudding-faced effigy of Droeshout ', by the contemplation of which he has declared himself so wofully depressed.

And yet every one did not declare against Droes-

PLATE 18

Mr. WILLIAM

SHAKESPEARES

COMEDIES,
HISTORIES, &
TRAGEDIES.

Publithed according to the True Originall Copies.

LONDON
Printed by Iſaac Iaggard, and Ed. Blount. 1623.

Title-page of the FIRST FOLIO, as issued
(Howard Staunton's Copy)

hout. A. van Huelle, in his life of Houbraken,[1] while highly praising the Dutch engraver's superb plate of the Chandos Shakespeare (1747) in Birch's *Heads of Illustrious Persons*, declares—' I greatly prefer to this romanticized bust the engraving of Martin Droeshout. There indeed we find the features which characterize the author of *Romeo* as well as of him who wrote *Julius Caesar*. What nobility in that forehead ! with what feeling is rendered the pensive and penetrating expression of the eyes and of the smile, of which the irony is softened by the sweetness of soul !' Here is appreciation if you like !

The title-page of the First Folio here reproduced is from Howard Staunton's copy (Plate 18). The dedicatory inscription ' TO THE READER ' which appears variously, in the different editions, opposite or below the print (and with numerous typographical varia- tions[2]) is Ben Jonson's evidence—for what it is worth —of the excellence of the likeness. We must not take this too seriously, perhaps, as this sort of tribute was in his day more or less *de rigueur* in the short poems with which it was the fashion to recommend portraits to the world. In France and Holland, as well as in England, in the seventeenth century, the best (and often the worst) poets were engaged to write eulo- gistic poems of the sort, irrespective of the artistic merit of the engravings. These verses were manu- factured to order, often without the plate being seen by the versifier, wherefore the value of the testimony as to excellence may easily be discounted. Yet it is more than likely that Jonson saw the first proof and hoped for the best, before Droeshout's further addi- tions compromised its reputation as a representation

[1] *Jacobus Houbraken et son Œuvre*, 1875.
[2] In the Third Folio there are no fewer than thirty-two such variations from the text of the First.

of humanity.   The meaning here is unmistakable.
Clearly, the lines

> Wherein the graver had a strife
> With Nature to out-do the life,

intentionally give an echo of what Shakespeare had
said thirty years before—in 1593—in *Venus and
Adonis* :—

> Look, when a painter would surpass the life,
> His art 's with Nature's workmanship at strife ;

and Dryden, fulsomely apostrophizing Kneller, repeated the idea as well as the form :

> Such are thy pieces, imitating life
> So near, they almost conquer in the strife ;

and the couplet is in a way echoed—down to the
Epilogue to *The Brothers* (1769) by Richard Cumber-
land, in the compliment to Sir Joshua Reynolds on
his picture of ' Garrick between Comedy and
Tragedy ', beginning—

> Who but hath seen the celebrated strife
> Where Reynolds calls the canvas into life.

Many other examples might be quoted, and of the
concluding lines of Ben Jonson's verse dozens of
parallels be given.   You remember them :

> O, could he but haue drawne his wit
> As well in brasse,[1] as he hath hit

---

[1] ' Brass ' and ' copper ' were terms synonymous in their application
to the plates on which engravers worked long after Shakespeare's
day.   An example may be found in John Evelyn's *Sculptura* of 1662.
In the list of contents is the entry : ' Engraving on Plates of Brass
for Prints when first appearing . . . 35.'   On referring to p. 35 we read :
' The Art of Engraving and working off, from Plates of Copper . . . was
not yet appearing, or born with us, till about the year 1490.'   Brass
is, of course, copper with zinc in it ; being harder than pure copper
it was largely used by engravers for book-plate printing.
  Again, we read in the advertisement of Nicholas Culpeper's work
(1670), ' The Anatomy of the Body of Man ; wherein is exactly
described the several parts of the Body of Man, illustrated with very
many larger *Brass Plates* than was ever in English before.'

His face ; the Print would then surpasse
All, that was euer writ in brasse.
But, since he cannot, Reader, looke
Not on his Picture, but his Booke.

The idea was already old. On Domenico Ghirlandaio's portrait of Giovanna Tuornabuoni, of 1488, a similar compliment, a paraphrase if one may call it so, is found : ' Art ! ' says the writer, ' if thou couldst render as well qualities of heart, and charm of mind, there would be no more beautiful picture in the world.'

Passing over such inscriptions as that under Albert Dürer's print of Melanchthon (1526)—

Viventis potuit durerius Ora Philippi, Mentem non potuit pingere
Docta Manus—

we come to Malherbe's verses under the portrait of Montaigne as engraved by Philippe de Leu, written probably about 1585 :

Voici du grand Montaigne une entière figure ;
Le peintre a peint le corps, et lui son bel esprit ;
Le premier, par son art, égale la nature ;
Mais l'autre la surpasse en tout ce qu'il écrit—

and may wonder if Ben Jonson imitated Malherbe or merely ' coincided ' with him.

Then, in 1618, appeared Simon Passe's print of Lancelot Andrewes, Bishop of Winchester (who, it will be remembered, was the general editor of the Authorized Version of the Bible), bearing beneath it the dedication signed by George Withers :

These Lineaments of Art, have well set forth
Some outwart features (though no inward worth)
But to these lines his writings added, cann
Make up the faire resemblance of a Man
For as the bodie's form is figured here
So there the beautyes of his Soule appeare.

(Under the same Bishop's portrait of 1657 is a variation of the same idea, ending with the lines—

> And now that grave Aspect hath deign'd to shrink
> Into this less Appearance. If you think
> 'Tis but a dead Face, Art doth here bequeath
> Look on the following Leaves and see him Breath.)

Again, below the younger Crispin van Pass's portrait of Francis Bacon is a bantering apostrophe to the engraver :

> *Graveur, le papier de ce liure*
> *Où Bacon a peint son Scauoir,*
> *Aura sur le temps ce pouuoir*
> *Qu'il durera plus longtemps que ton cuiure.*

And under ' The Portraicture of Captayne Iohn Smith Admirall of New England ', engraved by George Glover about the year 1617, is a verse containing the verses :

> These are the Lines that show thy Face but those
> That show thy Grace and Glory, brighter bee . . .
> So, thou art Brasse without but Golde within.

All these precede Droeshout.   A couple of examples will show that this sort of laudatory inscription usually retained the same central idea in the years that followed. The rhymester who in 1646 contributed the lines to Marshall's portrait of Sir John Suckling for *Fragmenta Aurea* apparently had Ben Jonson's lines in mind :

> Sucklin whose numbers could invite
> Alike to wonder and delight
> And with new spirit did inspire
> The *Thespian* scene and *Delphick* Lyre ;
> Is thus exprest in either part
> Above the humble reach of art ;
> Drawne by the Pencill here you find
> His forme, by his own Pen his mind.

And Sir Bulstrode Whitelock, who died in 1675, is

apostrophized with similar rapture scarcely convincing enough to carry off successfully the last shocking two lines of the ' poor Hexastick ' :

> To limne thy merits, and Heroick meedes
> Illustrious Whitlock is a task that needs
> A noble draught, for who dares be so bold
> To cut in Brasse what should be grav'd in Gold
> Or with one poor Hexastick raise ye columnes
> Of his vast merit which deserveth volumnes.

Whether or not Ben Jonson meant quite what he said—(he repentantly admits that he was formerly sometimes to blame in this matter)—the fact remains that the print was issued in an expensive memorial edition of Shakespeare's work, issued at £1 (say, some £6 or £7 of our money to-day) by Shakespeare's fellow-actors, and dedicated to two of the greatest noblemen of the realm, high personages at Court and in Society, who had known the Poet and were perfectly familiar with his appearance. It may therefore be believed—so many eyes being on him— that Jonson wrote with circumspection, with due regard to truth. As to the price of the book—does it not seem, with regard to the longish interval that elapsed before the next edition was called for—nine years—that it was the prohibitive cost of it that delayed the sales, and not, as some would have us believe, the public neglect of the man of Stratford ? How many of our leading dramatists' works—even to-day—when the authors have been dead for seven years (and retired for years before that) would ' go off ' quickly at from £5 to £10 per Folio ?

The print, as it is commonly known, was engraved by the year 1622 by Martin Droeshout who was an Englishman born. The faults in it spring at us at once, although they are not quite so obvious in the early impression from the plate. The forehead does

not show so badly as in later prints what Mr. Arthur
Benson has called the 'horrible hydrocephalous
development of the skull', yet it is singularly hard
and over-accentuated in the jaw line from the ear
downwards, which has actually suggested to some
of those who ache at all costs to discredit the portrait
as such, that it is a mask. Yet this same line appears
not only in many engravings, but in many oil
paintings of the period and since. For example,
it is quite as marked in Sir Joshua Reynolds's painting
of Richard Burke, at which I was looking not long
ago, to take only one case out of scores. The hair does
not balance on the two sides ; the ear is malformed ;
the cupid's-bow of the mouth, with its great depres-
sion of the medial lobe, is utterly contradictory of
the mouth in the bust. The mouth here is perhaps
the most deplorable defect in the head. As is very
obvious, it is too far to the right and has become a
deformity. Place your hand over it and after studying
the upper part of the face, withdraw your hand,
and you will see that it is not in the place in which
you would expect to find it—the fact being that it is
centred right below the nostril. In the 'Flower
portrait', which we shall presently consider, it is
corrected and placed in the proper position. There
is a strongly emphasized hatchet-like shape to the
lacrymal *fossa*; there is a hard long sweep of the eyebrows ; and the head is much too big for the body ;
while the exaggerated and distorted perspective
of the lines of the dress, as well as of the trimming of it, especially on the left (with the grotesquely
large and vilely drawn shoulder-'wings'), show
that this portion at least was not done from life.
As to these exaggerations, an American writer was
the first to declare that it made two left sleeves—
how is not apparent—and this tailor-authority has
been acclaimed with rapture and found followers

even here in England among the heterodox. I come
to that again.

But worst of all is the illumination of the head.
The light comes from more than one place—it falls
on the top of the head, right on to a strangely accentuated crescent-shape below the right eye-socket ;
it comes from the left of the nose, according to the
shadow on the right side of it, and on the ' wired-
band ', as this style of collar was called ; yet there is
shadow on the left of the left cheek, and light on
the edge of the hair on the right, which ought to
be in shade.   And, still more strange, the lights in
the eyes and the chief shadows on the face, are both
on the same side. All this is pretty conclusive that
the artist worked not from an oil painting, but from
an existing ' limning ' of the poet—a portrait con-
sisting of an outline drawing, with perhaps delicate
flat washes of colour—as in a Hilliard miniature
when miniatures were widespread in the art of
Elizabeth's day ; and that, when he was required to
strengthen it with added shadows and modelling, in
order to give life and force to an engraved plate, the
inexperienced young artist carried the plate as far
as he could—and carried himself over the border-
line of sane facial representation. To this same
conclusion, I find, Sir George Scharf (the first
Director of the National Portrait Gallery) also
arrived. But, when all is said, the outstanding fact
remains—that the forms of the skull, with its perpendicular rise of forehead, correspond with those in
the Stratford effigy : and this—the formation of the
skull—is the definitive test of all the portraits. The
Droeshout and the sculptured effigy show the skull
of the same man, who, in the engraving, is some
twenty years or so younger than him of the bust.

As to the bad drawing of the doublet and its
ornamentation—from which it has been attempted,

F

quaintly enough, to prove, cryptically, that it is the
back, or partially the back, and not the front—its
fault lies as much in its stiffness as in its lines. In
the portrait of Sir Walter Raleigh, painted about
1590 by Zuccaro, we see almost equal convergence
of the lines. Droeshout, indeed, was often abomin-
ably bad in his draughtsmanship, especially in his
perspective. In his plates of ' The Prophecies of
the Sybills ', the fifth of the series of twelve—
' Sybilla Samia '—holds a book so amazingly out of
perspective that it is hardly recognizable as a book
at all, so post-impressionistic is it in shape. His
figure of ' Springe ' (in the set of the Seasons) is
remarkable not merely for the similarity of treatment
in the Shakespeare portrait, but for the same bad
want of system of *chiaroscuro*.

If we would see the correct drawing of the costume
which Shakespeare wears, we may look at the portrait,
now in the National Portrait Gallery, of the broad-
chested Earl of Essex, painted in 1597, and we become
more indulgent towards young Droeshout (Plate 19).
It is reversed for the sake of comparison. The rich
dress has greatly puzzled many worthy commenta-
tors. It was that of gentlemen of ' the better sort '
of the day. We have it, in the same Gallery, in the
portrait of George Carew, Earl of Totnes, in Paul
Van Somers' Henry, Prince of Wales, and in others.
Henry, Marquess of Worcester, in the panel portrait
of him which was sold at Foster's auction-rooms on
March 13, 1913, wears a costume identical with that
in the Shakespeare engraving. It has been suggested
that the mere mummer Shakespeare would not have
worn such a doublet, unless he was in stage dress,
or in the uniform of the Duke's Players—either of
which surmises may be correct ; but it is perhaps
more likely—seeing the disparity in the relative proportions of head and body—that Droeshout, work-

PLATE 19

The EARL OF ESSEX
in the National Portrait Gallery
(Reversed for Comparison : showing
the costume correctly drawn)
(Copyright of Emery Walker)

The DROESHOUT PRINT
(First Folio)

(Copyright of Emery Walker)

PLATE 20

The 'FLOWER PORTRAIT'
Also (incorrectly) called 'The Droeshout Original'
By permission of the Trustees of the Stratford Memorial

ing from a limning of the head only, stuck it (and that too high) above the body he so infelicitously invented and so flatteringly attired.

We now revert to Droeshout ; and I point once more to the print—this time a heavier impression, well on in the edition of 500 copies or thereabouts which constituted the first issue of the Folio.

This brings us to the so-called ' Droeshout Original ', otherwise, and more properly and correctly, known as the ' Flower portrait ', presented in 1895 to the Shakespeare Memorial Gallery by Mrs. Charles Flower—a member of the Stratford family which founded that institution and has extended to it such munificent patronage (Plate 20.) Such history as the portrait has is altogether negative. Mr. Flower had bought it from the executrix of Mr. H. C. Clements of Sydenham, by whom it was alleged to have been presented to him by a descendant of Shakespeare's family, in whose possession it had been since the Poet sat for it. No names were given—no proofs offered, no evidence of the slightest kind vouchsafed. It all hangs on the bare assertion of the vendor. It is more or less the story, in its main lines, provided to support so many other so-called portraits of Shakespeare, and can well be ignored. We must rely for our conclusion on the portrait itself. An inscription on the back asserts that in the middle of the eighteenth century it was exhibited in London, and ' thousands went to see it ' ; but the most diligent research has failed to reveal any contemporary, or any other, mention of this important popular event ; which is the more curious as the feverish Shakespearian activity about that time, preceding the Bicentenary and Garrick's Jubilee, is fully reflected in the records of the time. The picture has been shown at the Crystal Palace and at the Alexandra Palace (where it was slightly damaged in the great fire). It was first brought into serious consideration when Dr. Lionel Cust introduced it to the attention of the Society of Antiquaries in 1895—when among the Fellows and leading Shakespearean scholars it made a few friends, and far more scornful enemies. The authorship of it was at one time absurdly ascribed—as so many Shakespeare portraits have been, quite at random—to Cornelis Janssen ; and the reason for the obscurity in which so important an object as an undoubted portrait of Shakespeare—from the life—had been allowed to remain, was that brought forward in defence of several other alleged portraits of the Poet : ' the Puritan ascendancy and civil wars '. A justification so weak does the work undeserved discredit.

The picture is painted on gesso on a worm-eaten panel of English elm, which had previously done service for a portrait of a lady in a high ruff and a red dress (as can be traced in a good light especially when the sun is shining on it). [What if it should be ' The Dark Lady ' ?] The costume worn by Shakespeare is simpler than in Droeshout's engraving, of which its adherents believe it to be the original. It has the appearance of tempera work ; and, if the allegations of those who examined it in 1895–6 that it contains megilp and bitumen, which, being still soft through freshness, yielded to Sir J. Charles Robinson's pin-test in the recent paint, are true—as they doubtless are—that might only prove recent restoration and extensive repair, and not necessarily imply entire imposture, as many asserted without, however, being able to carry general conviction.

The character of the picture—which may be a seventeenth-century production, executed from the print—is quite inconsistent with a portrait from life. There are none of those little tentative experimental touches which are invariably present, even in the

PLATE 21

The 'FLOWER PORTRAIT'

Showing the Painter's corrections of mistakes
and bad drawing by the Engraver

The DROESHOUT PRINT

(First Folio)

(Copyright of Emery Walker)

most dashing portrait, when an artist is exploring for the details about the eyes and corners of the mouth—the accidents of a face—which give expression, likeness, and life—the colour and folds of the skin and the play and forms of the muscles. There is just that deliberateness of execution, the boldness and firmness of handling, that we expect from the painter who, confident in his traced outlines, goes straight ahead on the design he has ' squared off ' from the authority before him, with nothing to find out—no problem to solve. Thus, the woodenness of the picture—precisely like that in a sign-painting—corresponds, as we might expect, to the hardness of the print. But the painter, who knew his business up to a point, has constantly departed from the original where it was obviously incorrect, and so has introduced many improvements.

An engraver, when he has his original before him, has to copy it, and not deliberately to introduce errors grossly departing from it. Yet every difference in form between picture and print is here to the advantage of the picture, and tends towards naturalness (Plate 21). The lighting of the head in the Print is unintelligible —rather, indeed, illogical ; in the Painting there is a broad system of illumination. The ridiculous crescent-shaped light under the eye is broken up and dispersed. What engraver, with such simple light-and-shade before him would plunge into the complicated contradictions of the Droeshout Print ? Why—we might ask—should he represent as a malformation the lobe of the ear well drawn in the picture ? Why systematically misrepresent the lacrymal *fossa* and caruncle of the eye—a characteristic defect of young Droeshout in his other engravings of heads ? Why put a light on the ear, which is in deep shadow ? Why exaggerate the arrangement of the hair, of *un*-horizontality ? Why play tricks with the shape of

G

the mouth—another of Droeshout's mannerisms ?—
all the ' Sybills ' sport the same intensified ' Cupid's
bow '. Why place this nearly full-face mouth in
a nearly three-quarter-face head ? Why cast undue
light on the wired band where it is in shade ? Why
make this serene forehead bulbous ? Why vitiate
the perspective of the dress by ignoring and falsifying
the almost perpendicular line of the central trimming
before him ? Why exaggerate the wings of the
sleeves ? And why, above all, suppress the one
piece of important evidence testifying that the
portrait is Shakespeare's—the inscription in the left-
hand corner of the picture—*Willm̃ Shakespeare,
1609* ? Why suppress *that* ? Why should the
engraver—how incompetent soever he may be—do
all these things, and introduce gratuitously all these
faults, if this alleged ' original ', without those faults,
were before him to trace and copy ? On the other
hand—is it not obvious ?—a fairly practised painter,
with a faulty original engraving to work from, would
not hesitate to put right the defects (as here has been
done), even to making the left eye match the right,
although with his uncompromising journeyman-
signboard sort of touch he gives a slightly aquiline
shape to the nose.

As to the inscription—it cannot be accepted as
contemporary with Shakespeare, in 1609. In an age
in which such inscriptions were common, this one
is unique among all the rest, in being written, in
neither capital nor in ' lower-case ' letters, nor even
in italics, but in cursive script. There is in it too,
an ' a ' which is modern—but that may possibly
be a repair and so should not, in fairness, be brought
forward in hostile witness. But there is something
more.

Everybody who was inclined to accept this picture,
or to dispute it, forgot the existence—or overlooked

PLATE 22

The Halliwell-Phillipps 'UNIQUE PROOF' of the Droeshout Portrait
(Now belonging to H. C. Folger, Esq., New York)
From the original Photograph in the Shakespeare Birthplace
By permission of the Trustees

PLATE 23

The HALLIWELL-PHILLIPPS 'UNIQUE PROOF'
From the Photograph supplied by H. C. Folger,
of New York
By permission of the Owner

the significance—of the so-called *Unique Proof* discovered in 1864 [1] by Halliwell-Phillipps (who paid
£100 for it), now the property of Mr. H. C. Folger (who
acquired it from Mr. Perry) in America (Plate 22). It
is this which supplies documentary proof of what has
hitherto been based on reasoning on artistic grounds
alone. This is here shown, in the first place, from the
photograph of it in the Shakespeare Birthplace, by
consent of the Trustees. In this witness-in-chief,
which, as I shall presently show, is far from impeccable, we see a more human face ; but the main
interest lies in a few minor but very significant
divergences.

It is no longer possible to call the proof ' unique '
as another exists in the Bodleian Library—and yet
another in the British Museum. There is said to
be still a fourth, known as the Lilly proof. [2]

The Halliwell-Phillipps photograph is introduced
here partly for the sake of completeness, but mainly
in order that I may make the *amende honorable* for
having publicly stated that the ' First Proof ' laid
down on the spurious title-page of the Malone First
Folio was a later state than this *Folger-Halliwell-
Phillipps* 'Unique Proof' (Plate 23). On receiving from
Mr. Folger the photograph I found to my amazement
that the photograph of it belonging to the Trustees
of the Birthplace is wholly misleading. I knew that
it was out of focus, but I did not know, and could
hardly guess, that the photograph was from an under-
exposed plate, and that that was the reason why
many lines do not appear in it. The absence of
these lines would naturally lead one to believe that

[1] Announced in the *Art Journal*, 1865, p. 30.
[2] The late Mr. Sabin informed me that in 1911 he bought at
Sotheby's auction-room a copy of the First Folio with the Droeshout
plate in the ' unique ' state, and that within two years he had sold it to
an American customer for £2,700 : the volume, he said, had a can-
celled leaf in the matter preceding *Troilus and Cressida*.

this Malone print is a later ' state ' (Plate 24). Even as
it is, the matter has given a good deal of trouble to
Sir Frank Short, the President of the Royal Society
of Painter-Etchers, and to me, to determine this
matter of ' states ', because photographs enlarged
six times have been necessary to prove that differences
which exist between the two good photographs (of
the Folger and Birthplace proofs) are not of ' line '
but really of more generous inking of the Malone plate
(Plate 25). In one case there is still doubt—whether
at the point of the collar it is increase of printing-ink,
or retouching with the burin, that has repaired the
blemish.

The matter seems a very trifling one to persons of
normal temperament ; but to the collector and to the
specialist connoisseur of engraving it is of prodigious
importance that a man would fight for to the death.

The Malone title-page on which this ' unique
proof ' is laid is here shown in order that the modern
—probably eighteenth century—printed page may
reveal its character to the spectator (Plate 26).

The early ' state ' of the head in the First Folio, now
spoken of as the *Quaritch Folio*—lately acquired by
the British Museum—is identical, except for minor
details and variations incident to the operation of
printing (Plate 27). It looks slightly woollier than
the others because it is reproduced (by the kindness
of Mr. Dring, of Messrs. Quaritch) from the excellent
half-tone rendering issued by the firm from whose
hands the volume passed into the National Collection. The fine mesh throws a glamour of softness
over the whole.

These, then, are the three known ' proofs '. Where
the Lilly proof may be—if it exists at all—is not
known.

Let us now run through the editions of the
Droeshout head, showing how the plate did service

PLATE 24

The MALONE PROOF

By permission of the Bodleian Library

PLATE 25

MR. WILLIAM
SHAKESPEARES
COMEDIES,
HISTORIES, &
TRAGEDIES.

Publiſhed according to the True Originall Copies.

LONDON
Printed by Iſaac Iaggard, and Ed. Blount. 1623.

The Genuine Malone Proof on the 18th-century printed
proof of the Title-page to the First Folio
By permission of the Bodleian Library

PLATE 26

From the Photograph, at the Birthplace, of the
Halliwell-Phillipps 'Unique Proof'

From Mr. Folger's photograph of the Proof

Enlargements of a Corner of the Collar in the two Proofs,
to illustrate the question of 'States'

PLATE 27

The BRITISH MUSEUM PROOF
(The line across the middle does not occur in the plate)
By Courtesy of Messrs. Quaritch

PLATE 28

Earliest Proof of the Title-page of the First Folio, with the
Halliwell-Phillipps 'Unique Proof' of the
Droeshout Portrait
By permission of H. C. Folger, Esq., New York

PLATE 29

The DROESHOUT PRINT
From the First Folio—1623 (the Turbutt Copy)
By permission of the Bodleian Library

PLATE 30

The D R O E S H O U T   P R I N T
From the Second Folio—1632
(With small lines from the pupils cutting into lids and extra line of hair,
detached, on the right on the back of the head)
By permission of the Bodleian Library

in the four (really five) editions, or impressions, and how each issue may be distinguished and identified.

There is now here presented—the first time, I believe, it has ever been thus shown—the historic whole ' *unique proof* ' title-page with its irregular type-setting and wording and defective centring (Plate 28). Priority must be claimed for it over the other two because the type-page has a *colon*, instead of a full-stop, after the word ' Copies '. This has been corrected in the British Museum copy and, of course, in the ordinary First Folio. The Malone printed title-page, being spurious, does not count.

Mr. Folger, after much entreaty, for the treasure was stored away and was almost inaccessible, kindly had it retrieved and had this photograph made for me.

The noteworthy points of Mr. Folger's proofs are :
Small moustache ; *clean* chin ; *light* eyebrows ; the right one (our right) *rising*, and *kinked*, the left one curved *down* at the extremity ; the hair growing naturally from the head ; *no shadow cast* by the head on the collar (or ' wired band ').

Malone Proof (Bodleian copy). The same, but more heavily inked.

First Folio, 1623 (Bodleian—the *Turbutt* copy) (Plate 29). *Large* moustache ; *stubbly* chin ; *darkened* eyebrows ; the right one a *clean sweep*, *drooping* at the end ; the left *raised* at the end ; hair lightened where it springs from the head, possibly to represent it growing grey, but in effect to make it look wig-like ; a shadow *cast* by the head on the collar.

Second Folio, 1632 (Bodleian) (Plate 30.) Plate deteriorating ; hair whiter ; *an extra line of hair* at the back of the head, showing against the background ; a *short line drawn from the white spot* in each pupil, cutting into the lid—more upward in the left eye than in the right. In some copies of the First

H

Folio (at the British Museum and at Cambridge) these lines appear ; in the Bodleian ' original '—the ' Turbutt '—copy they do not : proving that they were added on the plate while the printing of it was proceeding.

Third Folio, 1663 (Wadham College) (Plate 31). Plate more worn and badly inked. Line from left pupil no longer cuts into the lid.

Third Folio, Second Impression, 1664 (Bodleian) (Plate 32). No difference from the last, but better printing.

Fourth Folio, 1685 (Bodleian) (Plate 33). Violent cross-hatching over nearly the whole plate : forehead, nose, lips, moustache, cheeks, and chin, and hair, even on the cast shadow, the doublet, and part of the collar. Only the background escapes. All is vigorously seared across in various directions in the vain hope of bringing back force and life into the worn used-up plate. The early impressions were not so bad as the later ones, which are dreadful. There was little future hope for the plate. In the 1664 Folio and the Fourth Folio, the portrait is transformed into a frontispiece by being removed to the opposite page, in order to make room for the additional list containing *Pericles* and the six apocryphal plays generally supposed to be there attributed to Shakespeare. (The ascription is cleverly implied— but it is certainly not stated.)

When the Print and Proof are placed side by side, it is seen that the most eloquent differences are those in the eyebrows, the moustache, and the wired band, and the edge-illumination of the hair where it springs from the face.

In the *Proof* the eyebrows are light—the shading lines downwards from left to right ; in the *Print* they have been worked over and the lines are now upwards. In the *Proof* the right eyebrow is shorter ;

PLATE 31

The DROESHOUT PRINT
From the Third Folio—1663 Impression, at Wadham College
By Permission of the Warden

PLATE 32

The DROESHOUT PRINT
From the Third Folio—Impression of 1664
By permission of the Bodleian Library

PLATE 33

The DROESHOUT PRINT
From the Fourth Folio—1685
('Restored' with cross-hatching)
By permission of the Bodleian Library

PLATE 34

The 'FLOWER PICTURE'

The DROESHOUT PRINT

(For Comparison)

The DROESHOUT PROOF

in the *Print* lengthened. In the *Proof* the right eye-brow is fairly straightened to where the frontal bone joins the *columnar nasi* with the little ' kink ' or angle ; in the *Print* it is widened, arched, and runs into the nose with a bold curve.

In the *Proof* the moustache is thin and narrow ; in the *Print* it has been broadened and enlarged.

In the *Proof* there is no shadow cast on the collar ; in the *Print* there is shadow.

In the *Proof* there is no light where the hair springs from the head ; in the *Print* there is a light.

In the *Proof* the chin is clean, in the *Print* two days' growth of beard has been added—all, evidently, to lend age to the face, and to make Shakespeare more recognizable to those who remembered him in his later years.

Now—when we compare these prints with the painting, can we escape the conclusion (even if we wished to do so) that, in historical sequence, the proof came first, the print second, and the picture last ? Thus :

1. *Proof*—eyebrow light, short, and ' kinked ' ; *Print*, eyebrow dark, long, and sweeping ; *Picture*, eyebrow dark, long, and sweeping (Plate 34).

2. *Proof*—moustache small ; *Print*—moustache large ; *Picture*—moustache large.

3. *Proof*—no shadow on collar ; *Print*—shadow on collar ; *Picture*—shadow on collar.

4. *Proof*—no light on hair ; *Print*—light on hair ; *Picture*—light on hair.

5. *Proof*—no inscription ; *Print*—no inscription ; *Picture*—inscription.

Once more—is it not obvious that the order, as I have said, was Proof—Print—Picture ?

III

It is odd that at the time when Halliwell-Phillipps ' discovered ' his ' unique proof ' amid joyful congratulations, none of the zealous and watchful critics had ever noticed that the proof had not only been discovered before, but that an undisclosed engraver —whom I believe to have been E. A. Ashbee—had executed a beautiful little plate of it (Plate 35)— only about half the size of the original, yet wherein he reproduced every mark of the ' proof ' state, while securing a closeness of imitation, in every engraved line, that is truly surprising. The more remarkable, indeed, is this in a plate little more than half the area of the original—about $5\frac{1}{2}$ inches by $4\frac{1}{2}$. It was first issued in Bathurst's edition issued in 1773, and was used in larger size in the third (Reed's) edition of 1785—about eighty years before Halliwell-Phillipps delighted the literary world with the vaunted uniqueness of his title-page.

Below the portrait and the main inscription is the orthodox pronouncement—' Engraved from the original Portrait prefixed to the first edition of his Works, 1623, the only one which has any pretension to authenticity '. Presumably, therefore, the editor and artist controlled one of the two, or three, known extant copies of the First Folio with the plate in the proof state—and it occurred to neither of them to make any fuss whatever about it.

This Droeshout Print has naturally been often engraved, more or less faithfully, for the decoration of Shakespeare's works. The first of which mention should be made is that by William Marshall, rather poorly executed, in reverse, as a frontispiece to the unauthorized edition of Shakespeare's *Poems*, published in 1640—eight years after the appearance of the Second Folio (Plate 36). (This has been called

PLATE 35

Engraving [? by E. A. Ashbee] after the Malone 'Proof', 1773 and
1785 of Johnson and Steevens's Edition

PLATE 36

By William Marshall, 1640

Frontispiece to Shakespeare's *Poems*

Facsimiled by J. Swaine, 1824

PLATE 37

The Fates decree, that 'tis a mighty wrong
To Woemen Kinde, to have more Greife, then Tongue
Will: Gilbirson: John Stafford excud:

Frontispiece by William Faithorne to *The Rape of Lucrece* ... (1655)
Facsimiled by R. Sawyer, 1819

a copy after a lost original by John Payne ; all the authorities, following Walpole, have affirmed it. But, inasmuch as no one is known to have seen an impression of the supposed Payne print, it may be questioned if such has ever existed). It has been for the most part very well facsimiled five times—by J. Swaine, on steel, and by others—with or without the signature *W. M. Sculpsit* beneath the verses, and each renders with curious precision the hardness of the original. The wired band is too upstanding, the ' rays ' upon it are too much elaborated, and the head and face are too globular ; but a point of interest lies in the cloak over the shoulder and the sprig of bay-leaves in the hand, which are the ' authority ' taken for the introduction of these embellishments in several of the faked and fabricated portraits of Shake-speare extant, graphic and sculptural. Especially it may be noted that the moustache is done from the ' Proof ' —appropriate enough to the youthful poet ; and that the hair on both sides of the face is made horizontal.

More curious is the portrait in the plate, attributed on good grounds to William Faithorne, of which only five impressions are known to exist (Plate 37). It is the frontispiece to that extraordinarily rare little book, *The Rape of Lucrece. . . . By the incomparable Master of our English Poetry Will: Shakespeare. Thereunto is annexed ' The Banishment of Tarquin' . . . by J. Quarles*, and published in 1655—representing Lucretia stab-bing herself in the presence of her lord and husband Tarquinius Collatinus. It has been several times excellently copied from 1819 onwards ; this fac-simile is by R. Sawyer.

In the seventeenth century the Droeshout Print was necessarily the type of portrait adopted by the publishers until 1709 (when Tonson used also a version of the Chandos portrait for Rowe's edition of Shakespeare). It was employed also for the unimportant purposes of title-pages of this sort— the title of John Cotgrave's issue (with that name) of his *Witts Interpreter* of 1662 (Plate 38). The Droeshout Shakespeare here takes its place among the series of six great Englishmen and two Frenchmen—one of whom, Du Bartas, is represented with a crown of bays, so unmerited in his case, together with Shakespeare and Ben Jonson.

The portrait in this print—which was engraved by Hollar's pupil, Richard Gaywood—measures only about three-quarters of an inch each way, and yet a great enlargement does not diminish the character of the original.

This tiny scrap of homage to Shakespeare is often overlooked. It was repeated in the next edition of the book, nine years later, wretchedly copied by another hand ; but the volume was one of the more popular among the humbler collections and anthologies, mainly of a humorous sort, and there was little insistence on artistic excellence, or appreciation of it.

As far as is known, up to 1790 no fabrications of portraits of Shakespeare, painted with deliberate intent to deceive, were known. There were copies of the Droeshout and the Chandos portraits, and casts of the bust at Stratford and from the statue in Westminster Abbey ; but they were frankly admitted to be copies, or memorials. In 1790 Stockdale published the version by William Sherwin of the Droeshout Print, with improvements (Plate 39). [Sherwin was a bit of a character who, according to Nollekens, when he had to draw a figure, ' would begin at the toe and draw the figure upwards in a most correct and masterly manner'. The elder Henning—the sculptor of the Pan-Athenaic friezes on Burton's arch at Hyde Park Corner and on the Athenæum Club—did the same.] This print, issued as the frontispiece to

PLATE 38

The Droeshout type as adopted in John Cotgrave's
Witts Interpreter. Engraved by R. Gaywood, 1655

PLATE 39

Engraved by William Sherwin (1784 and 1790) to represent the
Droeshout Print with the falling moustache—precursor
of the Felton portrait

PLATE 40

The "'Robert' Elstracke" Portrait
(in pen and ink)
Adaptation of the Droeshout Portrait
By permission of Mr. Beatson Blair

PLATE 41

PAINTING CORRESPONDING TO THE 'UNIQUE PROOF'
By permission of Sir James Ranken Fergusson, Bart.

Ayscough's edition of Shakespeare of 1790, has only this in it to interest us—that it is the first graphic portrait—(recommended as ' a striking likeness ' by its publisher)—which shows the Poet as in the Droeshout Print, but with a *falling moustache*, thus heralding the advent of the Felton portrait.

This was in 1790—and two years later, in the course of nature, came the famous ' Felton ' portrait to light. The way had apparently been paved for it. It may be only a coincidence : on the other hand, even as a coincidence it is painfully suggestive. It aroused wide suspicion, for the Felton is the first painted portrait with a falling moustache. But that is another story.

Here, at least, we touch the borderland of the deliberate fakes—and spurious portraits of Shakespeare—of which an amusing example is the clever and elaborate pen-drawing in which the Droeshout head has been set on a body wearing a princely robe, and placed in much the same setting as that in which James I was painted (Plate 40). The inscription, in absurd rococo script, meant to be accepted as ancient, but found on other Shakespeare frauds, tells us that it is by *Robert Elstracke*—the agreeable forger not knowing that the R. of the artist's first name stood not for ' Robert ' but for Reynold. This drawing, done on a vellum-paper by a craftsman of the ability of James Minasi, belongs to Mr. Beatson Blair of Manchester. It is, I believe, generally unknown.

We now pass to another unpublished picture (Plate 41) which, were it pure, would be thought by many to claim parenthood of the Droeshout proof—for while it has the aquiline nose of the Flower portrait (whimsically called the ' Original ' at the Stratford Memorial Gallery), it alone gives us—among painted portraits—the small moustache of the ' Unique Proof ', the Cupid's-bow mouth, and the hatchet-shaped lacrymal *fossa*. But, alas—it displays that awkward, bungled ear which is a hall-mark of the Shakespeare picture-forger, Zincke. Moreover, the hair is of the luxuriant growth and fashion of the favoured Chandos portrait, not that of the Droeshout. The faker, apparently, has been at work on a genuine picture. There is the blotchiness due to old repairs which have ' gone down ' in colour since they were poorly done a century and more ago. The portrait consisted originally of a head only ; by later additions it has been transformed into a bust-piece. Both the collar and doublet are compromises between the Droeshout and the Chandos ; but the most disturbing element is the quality of the broken colour in the flesh which we do not identify with English sixteenth or early seventeenth-century portrait-painting : it suggests a Flemish hand working on an English foundation.

This interesting work belongs to Sir James R. Fergusson of Spitalhaugh, West Linton, who acquired it in London many years ago ; but its history has not yet been traced. It is with his consent that it is here shown. On the back of the panel—which is certainly 300 years old and more—cut with an adze, before planes were in common use—is a beautifully incised inscription which leaves us unconvinced as to the date of it—[— W. S. 1616–]—especially as the lettering has been blackleaded—presumably in order to conceal the fresh colour of the excision.

Five more portraits I would touch rapidly upon, for they are closely allied to our subject ; two of them collated works, as it were ; two of them frankly imaginary presentations ; and the last a poet's ' vision '.

The first of these is in the fine plaque by Professor Lantéri, executed after the design of William Martin, LL.D., F.S.A., affixed to the wall of Barclay's

PLATE 42

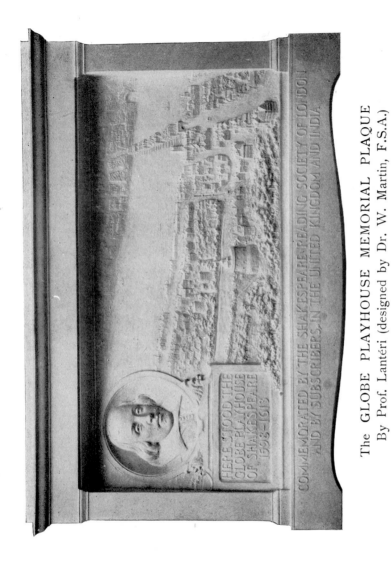

The GLOBE PLAYHOUSE MEMORIAL PLAQUE
By Prof. Lantéri (designed by Dr. W. Martin, F.S.A.)

PLATE 43

The First Design—with the Chandos Head

The SHAKESPEARE MEMORIAL IN SOUTHWARK
CATHEDRAL.
Droeshout type. By Henry McCarthy

Brewery (by the Shakespeare Reading Society in 1909), on, as was then believed, the site of the Globe Theatre by Bankside (Plate 42). This assumption has now been disproved by Mr. George Hubbard, F.S.A.[1] Here the Droeshout head is the source of inspiration, humanized in the realization of it. The sculptor, not without ' authority ', has exaggerated the space between the Globe and the river, and has set Old London Bridge where the present bridge now stands —a few yards to the west.

In 1912 a companion memorial to the honour of ' William Shakespeare for several years an inhabitant of this parish' was erected in Southwark Cathedral, mainly through the efforts of Dr. Ralph W. Leftwich supported by the generosity of Mr. Sanford Saltus, an American lover of the Poet (Plate 43). Beneath a Tudor Gothic canopy, against a background setting forth the Cathedral, the Globe Playhouse, and other buildings along Bankside—together with the southern arch of London Bridge decorated with impaled heads of malefactors, the recumbent Shakespeare reclines, as the sculptor says, ' meditating his plays '. It is a sympathetic rendering by Mr. Henry McCarthy, executed in alabaster, the material commonly used for ecclesiastical effigies in Shakespeare's day. The portrait is very cleverly realized, a good rendering of the Droeshout engraving. The first sketch—here set forth—which was shown to me by Dr. Leftwich was based upon the Chandos portrait. I pleaded for the Droeshout on grounds of authenticity and the suggestion was happily accepted.

The next—a very different work—is the extraordinarily original statue by the brilliant American sculptor, Mr. Frederick W. MacMonnies, done in

[1] See *On the Site of the Globe Playhouse of Shakespeare* . . . By George Hubbard, F.S.A., V.-P., R.I.B.A., Cambridge University Press, 1923.

K

bronze, based equally on the Droeshout Print, but slightly modified, he told me, by the study of the Stratford Bust (Plate 44).   This very impressive, and at the same time amusing, work now embellishes the Congressional Library in the Capitol at Washington, one of the several noble figures that look down, dominating the vast hall, and in good keeping with its refined enrichments.

Professor Charles J. Allen's bust, which crowns the Heminge and Condell memorial in St. Mary the Virgin Churchyard in Aldermanbury—dignified and convincing beyond most of the sculptured effigies of the Poet, and perhaps the most satisfactory head of its class in England—does honour to the two men to whom, we must suppose, we owe the First Folio (Plate 45).   It, too, is a happy amalgam of the Stratford Bust and the Droeshout Print—both of them immortalized in verse in the Folio itself, which is represented in the monument.   The characteristic shape of the skull in the Stratford Bust is well reproduced.   My photographs were taken from the plaster when the work was still in the studio.   This, probably, is what Garratt Johnson was trying to do.

Similarly inspired—but not, however, leaving wholly out of account the Janssen, Chandos, and Hunt likenesses of Shakespeare, in spite of their relative unworthiness—is the finely-realized ideal portrait by Ford Madox Brown, now one of the honoured ornaments of the Manchester Gallery (Plate 46).   Yet when this beautifully conceived and elaborated work was exhibited, in 1850, it was received with silence by artists, press, and public alike.   Madox Brown told me so, and added that Dante Rossetti sat to him for the picture—just as he himself had, most appropriately, posed to himself for his figure of Milton.   As Madox Brown himself wrote of the picture in 1865—it is ' an attempt to supply the want

PLATE 44

STATUE OF SHAKESPEARE

By FREDERICK W. MACMONNIES

At the Congressional Library in the Capitol, Washington

By permission of the Sculptor

PLATE 45

The STRATFORD BUST
for comparison with
the profile by Prof. Allen

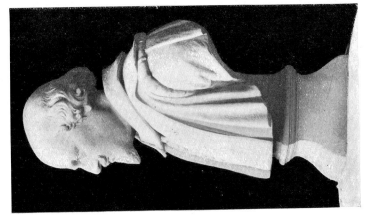

The BUST OF SHAKESPEARE
on the Heminge and Condell Memorial,
St. Mary the Virgin Churchyard, Aldermanbury
By Professor C. J. Allen, R.B.S.

PLATE 46

Portrait of
WILLIAM SHAKESPEARE
(The Stratford Bust and the Droeshout Print collated)
By FORD MADOX BROWN
By permission of the Manchester Corporation Art Gallery

PLATE 47

The 'VISIONARY' PORTRAIT OF SHAKESPEARE
By WILLIAM BLAKE, 1804
By permission of the Manchester Corporation Art Gallery

of a creditable likeness of our national poet, as a historian recasts some tale told long since in many fragments by old chroniclers '. According to William Rossetti, his son-in-law, this picture may be considered the first work done by the artist which shows a rather marked affinity to the methods of the Pre-Raphaelite Brotherhood which had been established in 1848. In a later manner Madox Brown executed two cartoons of the whole standing figure—to symbolize the Drama—intended for William Morris & Co. to execute in glass for Peterhouse College, Cambridge—a design—but the design was never carried into effect.

Finally, we have the realization by William Blake (Plate 47) of what he believed he saw when he was with Hayley at Felpham in 1801 to 1804—when he wandered on the sea-shore, and in his ' visions ' he ' saw the sands peopled by a host of souls—majestic shadows '—and then he painted some of them : Shakespeare, Homer, Milton, Dante, and the rest—his only pictures in tempera, almost in monochrome, all now at Manchester.[1] Blake claimed to have held converse with Shakespeare on this occasion, and affirmed, with genuine if whimsical sincerity—' He is exactly like the old engraving which is said to be a bad one. *I* think it very good.'

And thus he unconsciously realized for himself the Droeshout Print, which he already knew well, and with it, visions from *Hamlet* and *Macbeth*. But he never explained what Shakespeare, Homer, and the rest of the mighty throng were doing on Felpham sands. It will be seen that in this beautiful and sympathetic head Blake—himself not always a very precise draughtsman—has corrected the worst errors

---

[1] This, together with the eighteen other portraits of poets—English, foreign, and ancient—were intended for a frieze in William Hayley's library.

of Droeshout ; and that, while making it human, he insistently retains that clear line of the jaw from ear to chin, which recent enemies of the dramatist of Stratford fatuously declare to be a proof that Shakespeare wears a mask.

My demonstration is at an end, although there is much more I should like to set forth here. We have advanced, perforce, into what is, rather absurdly, the arena of controversy, although in regard to our two portraits there is really no room for dispute. We have considered these two portraits pretty closely, for they stand together and cannot fully be judged apart. We have followed them through 300 years, and, weighing all the circumstances and all the points which have been set forth, we may rest assured that we have had pictured to us, quite truly in the main, the presentment of Shakespeare, Man and Poet, as he lived and worked.

INDEX

L